D1437272

Also available in this series from Quadrille:

the little book of
TIDINESS

Edited by
Alison Davies

quadrille

*"Order and tidiness is
the first law of Heaven."*

BRUNELLO CUCINELLI

Everyone has swept something under the carpet at some point in life and allowed cobwebs to creep into corners. When it comes to tidiness, however, there is a lot to be said for dusting off the vacuum and having a spring clean. A tidy house means a tidy mind after all, and both are key to a calm, happy and decluttered life.

Dictionary definition of 'tidiness':

The state or quality of being arranged neatly and in order.

Treat tidiness with respect. See it as a tool to free your mind from worry and your home from clutter, not as a chain to shackle or restrict you.

Being tidy is about being organized and neat so that you can manoeuvre physically and mentally with ease. It's a personal thing, and up to each individual as to how they monitor this and what works for them. Problems arise when we take a step too far in either direction. Those who never tidy tend to harbour clutter and live in a permanent state of confusion, while those whose need for order becomes obsessive tend to tidy every last bit of themselves and their life away. Both ends of the spectrum can cause an array of issues, including anxiety, stress, procrastination and problems with interpersonal relationships.

"My tidiness, and my untidiness, are full of remorse and complex feelings."

NATALIA GINZBURG

'Dilemma'

The world is divided,
they say, into two
personality types,
one of them being you:

1. Scattered papers on chairs
   hiding pens that are lost
   and the old sticky sweet
   that you hid to your cost.

2. Arty objects aligned
   on the bare window ledge
   exactly two inches
   from each perfect edge.

You both have a burden
you're destined to carry
and I can't decide which
I'd sooner not marry.

VIV APPLE

There are no right or wrong answers to how you should tidy.

Some people thrive in an organized mess, while others require everything to have a place.

Sense which personality fits best with you and be true to yourself. If you prefer the chaos then test out a more organized way of life, and if you are more ordered, try to be a little more open and carefree about tidying.

"Time and space – time to be alone, space to move about – these may well become the great scarcities of tomorrow."

EDWIN WAY TEALE

Tidiness gives us the chance to just take a moment in a world that is often cluttered. Our own small space of calm is something we may not appreciate when we have it – but will miss when it is buried under dirty laundry and work emails.

"Plan you progress carefully; hour-by-hour, day-by-day, month-by-month. Organized activity and maintained enthusiasm are the wellsprings of your power."

PAUL MEYER

What does being tidy mean to you?

Everyone has different wants and needs. What makes one person feel comfortable could prove to be too restrictive for another.

Find your place when it comes to tidiness and create reasonable guidelines that you can stick to.

**Questions to help you
on your tidiness journey:**

Are you happy in your environment?

Do you feel comfortable in your
environment?

Do you know where things are,
or are you constantly losing
important items?

Does your home bring you peace
and a sense of calm?

Do you constantly feel on edge or confused when you survey your surroundings?

Do you often enjoy spending time in other people's homes rather than your own?

Do you have a favourite space in your home?

Visualize an empty room in your mind. The unlimited space means you can move around freely.

You are the centre of the room.

You are the focal point.

Wherever you look there is only more room for you to inhabit.

Tidiness is not a rule to adhere to and neither is it set in stone. It's a tool that frees you and enables you to see limitless possibilities.

Tidiness around the world

Compiled in 2014, the Mercer Global Financial list of the world's cleanest cities cites Calgary in Canada as the cleanest, most clutter-free city in the world. It is closely followed by Adelaide, Honolulu, Minneapolis and Kobe.

Singapore has some of the strictest anti-litter laws in the world, with escalating fines, community service orders and litter-dropping lectures. Repeat offenders will also find themselves wearing a sign that says "I am a litter lout".

*"Be strong in body,
clean in mind,
lofty in ideals."*

JAMES NAISMITH

Strength doesn't come from what you can do.

It comes from overcoming the things you once thought you couldn't.

"Organizing is what you do before you do something, so that when you do it, it is not all mixed up."

A. A. MILNE

To be constantly presented with a muddle of untidiness sends an unhealthy message to the subconscious mind. It reinforces feelings of confusion, making it impossible to make sense of the world around you.

25-day minimalism challenge

1. Purge your wardrobe
2. Clean out your handbag
3. Toss old socks out
4. Get rid of unused digital devices
5. Empty your wallet
6. Say no to something
7. Donate old books
8. Don't wear makeup for one day
9. Meditate today
10. Spend time with loved ones
11. Make a gratitude log
12. Evaluate your last 5 purchases
13. Stay offline for a day

14. Don't spend any money for 24 hours

15. Don't complain all day and make an effort to smile at people

16. Go out without your phone

17. Venture outdoors

18. Create a relaxing space

19. Re-evaluate your to-do list

20. Declutter your storage

21. Empty your junk drawer

22. Turn off notifications

23. Batch-cook your meals

24. Tidy your desk

25. Take a moment to appreciate your surroundings

Life does not always go to plan

You can't predict what is around the corner, but you can be prepared for it by being in a good place mentally and emotionally.

A tidy mind leaves you free from the debris of worry and able to think clearly. It means you have the space to manoeuvre and see a way through any problems that arise.

One of the best ways to achieve a tidy mind is by being self-aware and removing the clutter from your life.

Simply facing the mass of litter you've accumulated becomes overwhelming, and could ultimately cause you to disconnect completely.

Give yourself the freedom to breathe and move physically, and you'll be able to follow suit emotionally.

Consider your consumption

We live in a time in which we are constantly bombarded with adverts telling us what we need. In reality there are very few things we actually need and often we buy on impulse, based on how the item makes us feel. We continue to shop to make ourselves feel better, but instead become overwhelmed and weighed down by the accumulation of stuff.

Defeat the shopper's itch.

Next time you are in a shop, be conscious of why you are lusting after or feel the need to purchase certain things.

Try and consider the following:

Is it something you want or is it something you need?

What feelings you are trying to create?

What are you trying to distract yourself from by buying?

Can you afford it?

"One way to organize your thoughts is to tidy up, even if it's in places where it makes no sense at all."

URSUS WEHRLI

For every item you possess, ask yourself three questions:

- Do I really need this?

- Have I used/worn this within the past year?

- If I was running from a burning building, would I take this with me?

If the answer is 'no' to all three, then it's time to get rid of it.

If you answered 'no' twice, then give some serious thought to getting rid of it.

If you answered 'no' once, then put it on the reserve list for your next clear-out.

"Effective tidying involves only three essential actions. All you need to do is take the time to examine every item you own, decide whether or not you want to keep it, then choose where to put what you keep. Designate a place for each thing."

MARIE KONDO

If something no longer has a use, get rid of it. If something can be stored away neatly, then give it a home instead of discarding it where you stand.

Turn all the hanging clothes in your wardrobe around so that the hangers are facing the wrong way.

Everytime you take something out of your wardrobe to wear, replace it with the hanger back in its correct position.

If, after a year, there are any hangers still facing backwards, you need to take these items of clothing to a charity shop.

Clearing unnecessary items out of your life reduces clutter and makes you appreciate and value the things you do have.

Household chores are often a battleground for resentment and miscommunication. Sometimes we live with people who don't share our opinions on how tidy or clean a space should be. It can be hard to take a step back and understand that everyone has a different cleanliness threshold.

Here are some helpful tips to avoid future conflict:

- Be patient – acknowledge that it is a matter of priority and not of character.

- Have a conversation – talking through these differences is often the key to getting on the same page.

- Define it – sit down together and discuss what dirty, messy and clean mean to each of you.

- Compromise – create a distinction between personal and shared spaces.

- Get practical – make a list of household jobs and allocate chores accordingly.

- Motivate – schedule a few hours of cleaning, then reward yourself by spending time in your newly cleaned space eating or playing a game together.

" Clutter is not just the stuff on your floor – it's anything that stands between you and the life you want to be living."

PETER WALSH

Clutter attracts clutter.

Calm attracts calm.

"Clutter is the physical manifestation of unmade decisions fuelled by procrastination."

CHRISTINA SCALISE

Take before and after photographs of the space you're going to tidy. The 'before' picture will help you see the room objectively, making it easier for you to spot problem areas of clutter and congestion. The 'after' picture will give you a sense of accomplishment and remind you what can be achieved by being tidy.

"Don't let the perfect be the enemy of the good. Lower the bar. Actually spending ten minutes clearing off one shelf is better than fantasizing about spending a weekend cleaning out the basement."

GRETCHEN RUBIN

Set standards, but don't set them too high. Start small and build upon this. Tidiness is the result of organization and arrangement.

Some people are visual and panic if they can't see their belongings, but there is a solution. Things can be placed in neat piles, or put away in baskets and boxes, which can be kept close to hand. This way, they're organized and have a designated space, but they're still available and easy to see.

"People mix up cleaning with organizing. Being clean is a visual thing, but being organized is being able to find things when you need them."

JULIE MAHAN

"One may walk over the highest mountain one step at a time."

BARBARA WALTERS

You wouldn't expect to climb a mountain in a day. Instead you'd create a schedule that you could stick to, with achievable goals.

Treat cleaning and tidying the same way. Have a list of targets each day and work through them methodically. This helps to promote motivation, because you can see and feel that you are getting somewhere.

Tidying, like mountain climbing, is about the journey and the final destination.

Tidy plan

- Start by dissecting the area that you want to tidy into regions, so if you're aiming to tidy your entire house then pick a room. List the regions on separate pieces of paper.

- Split each region into sections, so you might have the area near the window, the area surrounding the fireplace, the area near the door, etc., and write these on the relevant piece of paper.

- Make a list of everything in each area, then pick one item at a time to clear.

- Remain focused and set yourself a time limit to clear the area; this way you'll be less likely to get distracted and abandon the process.

- Celebrate your victories. Every time you clear a space, acknowledge your achievement. Mark it off your list and be proud that you've achieved something.

"Fail to plan, plan to fail."

WINSTON CHURCHILL

"When we clear the physical clutter from our lives, we literally make way for inspiration and 'good, orderly direction' to enter."

JULIA CAMERON

If I could just get organized

There may be nothing wrong with you
The way you live the work you do,
But I can surely plainly see
Exactly what is wrong with me.
With you there may be nothing wrong,
But here's my trouble all along
I do the thing that don't amount
To very much with no account.
It isn't that I'm indolent
or dodging duties quite intent
I work as hard as anyone
And yet I get so little done
I nibble this, I nibble that
but never finish what I'm at.
The morning goes the noon is near
Before I know the night is here.

And all around me I regret
The things I haven't finished yet.
If I could just get organized
I oftentimes may realize
Not all that matters is the man
The man must also have a plan
It really seems important though
I let a lot of matters go
and all around me I neglect
the things I haven't finished yet.
I work as hard as anyone
And yet I get so little done
I'd do so much you'd be surprised
If I could just get organized.

BAIDURYA MUKHERJEE

Tidiness comes in many forms and detoxing is a good place to start.

It's time to wipe the slate clean and freshen up your life.

"Let's detox our cluttered academic brain. That's what the poet does. People call it daydreaming, detoxing our minds and taking care of that clutter. It's being able to let in call letters from the poetry universe."

JUAN FELIPE HERRERA

"Out of clutter, find simplicity."

ALBERT EINSTEIN

Tidiness doesn't only relate to the objects you see in front of you. Clutter can fill up all aspects of life and it's important to pinpoint these different areas.

Clear the clutter mentally

Imagine your mind is a room filled with cardboard boxes stacked from floor to ceiling.

Each box represents an area of life, and within them are more boxes which represent any worries, concerns or stresses relating to that area.

Visualize a rubbish chute, leading out from the room, which joins up to your mouth and allows you to breathe.

Picture yourself throwing each box down the chute. As you do this, take a deep breath in then breathe out, holding for four long counts.

See the room that is your mind gradually empty until all that's left is a huge white space with windows that you can finally see out of. Imagine this room filled with bright sunshine. See the windows open and imagine an invigorating breeze sweeping through the room.

Keep breathing deeply and enjoy the feeling of purity and space.

Repeat this visualization once a week to clear any mental clutter.

"Everybody gets so much information all day long that they lose their common sense."

GERTRUDE STEIN

It is easy to let mental clutter accumulate in the form of thoughts, fears and worries. All these thoughts can get in the way of our lives, pulling us out of the present moment.

Be aware of what distracts you from your purpose and make intentional decisions about whether to let those thoughts interrupt your day.

Put down your phone
and pick up your life.

Live intentionally.

Challenge yourself to a digital detox

Go without your gadgets for just one day. Experience the freedom of being completely hands-free, off the grid and offline.

How does it feel to move through the day being fully aware, not to be weighed down by the demands of emails, tweets, texts?

How does it feel to be free, disconnected from technology but connected to the world?

Extend the challenge to two days and so on until you feel you've truly embraced peace.

"*There are uncountable hours lost each year in the workplace because of disorganization.*"

JULIE MAHAN

"An individual may be an expert in any field but without inner cleanliness his brain is like a waste desert."

SRI SATHYA SAI BABA

"Be careless in your dress if you must, but keep a tidy soul."

MARK TWAIN

When we disconnect digitally, we reconnect emotionally. We become more personable. Our communication skills improve, which has a positive effect on our relationships.

We rethink our priorities.

We move more.

See more.

Enjoy more.

Live in the moment.

"When you sit at your desk, if you're lucky, there's a moment when you feel empowered to be someone or something else, to leap into another skin."

JOHN UPDIKE

Tidy Desk = Tidy Mind =
Tidy Work = Tidy Reward!

If you want to stay focused and impress at work, then it's a good idea to keep your desk tidy. Even if you don't have much room, you can keep it clutter-free which will leave you with more energy and clarity to deal with any tasks. This in turn helps you appear more confident, competent and professional.

"First comes thought; then organization of that thought into ideas and plans; then transformation of those plans into reality."

NAPOLEON HILL

- Start by treating your desk like a blank canvas. You are the artist and you're about to create a masterpiece. Whatever you include in the picture has to be worthwhile, of use and essential to your work life.

- Store your tools correctly. Keep pens and pencils in an easy-to-reach pot. Put papers together or in files and stack them in order.

- Have an in-tray for post and any incoming work, and an out-tray for things that you have dealt with and that need filing away. Make sure you devote ten minutes at the end of every day to clearing the out-tray.

- Remove any personal items. As lovely as it is to have mementos and reminders of home, they add to the clutter and can ultimately cause a distraction.

- Keep a waste-paper bin by your feet and use it. Spend five minutes every day going through the items on your desk and relegating those you no longer need to the bin.

- Spread upwards not outwards. If possible, have your computer monitor on a stand, and add extra shelving space so that you can store folders, files and anything that might otherwise clutter your desk.

"A garden requires patient labour and attention. Plants do not grow merely to satisfy ambitions or to fulfil good intentions. They thrive because someone expended effort on them."

LIBERTY HYDE BAILEY

Tidy garden

While it's easy to keep on top of clutter in your home and workspace, this can be more difficult to maintain with outdoor space. The garden, for many, is a place of recreation. It's a beautiful space in which to relax, connect with nature and destress after a hard day. Which is why it's just as important to sustain some kind of order and flow. It helps if you can treat outside space as another room, but while you might be more regimented with the interior of your home, you can give nature a free rein and work with it to create a balanced, tranquil area full of natural beauty.

The Japanese have always embraced tidy gardens, favouring blank space, carefully raked gravel paths and delicate plants.

From this the garden becomes a meditative, calm space.

"What a gift of grace to be able to take the chaos from within and from it create some semblance of order."

KATHERINE PATERSON

> *"Gardens are not made by singing 'Oh, how beautiful,' and sitting in the shade."*

RUDYARD KIPLING

It's time to roll up your sleeves and get a bit dirty in your efforts for tidiness. Think of gardening as therapy: sunshine, exercise and sense of acheivement do wonders for the soul.

Declutter your garden and enhance its natural beauty.

- Find a place to keep garden tools, such as a shed or outhouse. Smaller garden tools can be packed away in a box.

- Go on leaf and weed patrol. Make a point of checking your lawn and borders for errant leaves or weeds. Devote a chunk of time to this every week and you'll ensure a clear, clean and vibrant garden.

- Split your garden into sections and have allotted areas for entertaining, relaxing, growing fruit and vegetables, etc.

- If you have the room, create a wildflower area and let nature take over. In this space, sow wildflower seeds and plant bushes that provide shelter and food for local wildlife. This area gives your garden a sense of balance, allowing scope for order and creative abundance, which work together to support the environment.

- Even if you don't have a garden, there are things you can do. Hang pressed floral artwork in clear frames to allow the walls to shine through and to avoid bulky planters filling up your rooms.

Order, both inside and outside, is key to a calm existence.

Whether you're green-fingered or not,
when you see your garden thriving,
you will in turn thrive yourself.

Tidiness brings satisfaction.

"I enjoy the cleaning up – something about the getting of things in order for winter – making the garden secure – a battening down of hatches perhaps... It just feels right."

DAVID HOBSON

Tidy your worries away!

"Worry is interest paid on trouble before it comes due."

WILLIAM RALPH INGE

Worry fills the mind with litter.

Why would you want to stuff your head full of rubbish?

*"Better keep yourself clean and bright;
you are the window through which you
must see the world."*

GEORGE BERNARD SHAW

Worry litter

Take a large sheet of paper. Divide it into squares by drawing lines. Each square represents an area of your life. List any worries or fears relating to each area in the corresponding square.

Ask yourself, 'What is the worst that could happen to me if I discard this fear?'

Life still goes on.

The sun still rises and sets. In most cases the fear will never be realized, it's simply there cluttering up your mind, taking up important space and weighing you down with its presence. Once the page is filled, either rip it up into tiny pieces and throw it in the recycling, or shred it.

Tidiness and health

Research has shown that keeping your house tidy and clutter-free can also improve your health. This is because housework is an activity that gets the heart pumping. Those who would otherwise shun exercise might instead opt to clear the clutter, and while doing so reap the benefits of being active.

"Health is a state of complete harmony of the body, mind and spirit."

B.K.S. IYENGAR

Cleanliness

All-endearing cleanliness,
Virtue next to godliness,
Easiest, cheapest, needfull'st duty,
To the body health and beauty;
Who that's human would refuse it,
When a little water does it?

CHARLES AND MARY LAMB

"He longed for cleanliness and tidiness: it was hard to find peace in the middle of disorder."

ROBIN HOBB

"Joy is not in things;
it is in us."

RICHARD WAGNER

Clutter leads to stress and anxiety. Studies repeatedly show that hoarders and those who accumulate 'material things' struggle with higher levels of stress. Those who prefer a simpler, more streamlined approach to living find life much easier and more joyful.

"You may not know it, but at the far end of despair, there is a white clearing where one is almost happy."

JOAN BAEZ

Discard everything that doesn't bring joy into your life. Consider thoughts as well as objects.

"Some of us think holding on makes us strong; but sometimes it is letting go."

HERMANN HESSE

Rate your anxiety

If the thought of removing all your clutter makes you feel uncomfortable, treat it as a process.

Consider each object you'd like to get rid of and give it an anxiety rating from 1 to 10. 1 means it's ok, you might feel uneasy but you can cope; 10 means you feel distraught and full of grief at the thought of living without it. Aim to get rid of objects that are within the 1-4 range to start with.

Gradually increase this range as you go along. Over time, as you are more exposed to these feelings, you'll notice a shift in the way you think and feel. You'll see that getting rid of certain items and clearing the clutter can feel good.

"*The secret of change is to focus all of your energy, not on fighting the old, but on building the new.*"

SOCRATES

"When I let go of what I am,
I become what I might be.
When I let go of what I have,
I receive what I need."

LAO TZU

"Good health and good sense are two of life's greatest blessings."

PUBLILIUS SYRUS

If every item you own, every piece of junk that you hold on to for a reason, is special, then *nothing* is special. Learn to distinguish between that which is irreplaceable, and that which is habit.

"The cleaning is something I use as a reward if I get some work done. I go into a very happy state of mind when I'm vacuuming."

JOYCE CAROL OATES

Vigorous cleaning and tidying boosts mental health, relieving symptoms of depression. This is due to the balance of physical activity and seeing the benefits of a clutter-free environment. It's empowering to see the results of your efforts. It reinforces a sense of satisfaction and joy at having achieved a goal and ticked something off your 'to do' list. Those who engage in regular tidying are also able to unwind and relax more because they've created the perfect space in which to do this.

"He who buys what he does not need steals from himself."

SWEDISH PROVERB

Learn to live with less and you'll experience more!

"Things don't really impress me.
Memories impress me.
It's not the toys, it's the people."

R.A. SALVATORE

While we should consume mindfully, be aware that some experiences are gained through owning things.

If you buy a bike, for instance, you can gain a new sense of freedom and many great experiences while riding it.

It's all about finding the right balance for you.

Think in terms of memories. You can have thousands of memories that you treasure and that bring joy, but they do not make your home untidy.

Objects initially make you feel happy, but this is a fleeting emotion. As each item becomes outdated, the novelty is replaced by a need for something new.

In our hunger to fill the void we accumulate more and more stuff, until our world is cluttered with things that have no real meaning.

Memories have meaning and wonder. They can be plucked from the deepest corner of the mind and enjoyed at any time.

They may become old, but they're never outdated because they're unique to us, and a map of who we are.

They don't take up space because the brain cleverly stores them away.

They don't cost money, and if they're good ones they make you feel richer every time you relive them.

Make memories, and enjoy them again and again.

Create a memory box.

It will help you organize and keep safe those precious mementos that you do want to hold on to, and remind you of the importance of living.

When you feel the urge to splurge on more clutter, dip into your memory box. Pull out a memento, a photo, a shell gathered on the beach, a favourite poem or phrase, a ticket stub from your misspent youth, and revel in the memory.

Replay it in your mind like a film and experience the emotions again. By the time you've finished, the need for more should have waned.

"In plain words, chaos was the law of nature, order was the dream of man."

HENRY BROOKS ADAMS

"The journey of a thousand miles begins with one step."

LAO TZU

You'll never change your life until you change something you do daily. The secret to success can often be found in your daily routine.

> *"Simplicity is the ultimate sophistication."*

LEONARDO DA VINCI

"We really should consider very carefully whether we constantly need new things. I have been arguing for a long time for less, but better things."

DIETER RAMS
from *Kinfolk* issue Twenty-three

"Something I like to do a lot is just sit by water when there's a current and just stare into the water. I don't fish, I don't hunt, I don't scuba, I don't spear, don't boat, don't play basketball or football – I excel at staring into space. I'm really good at that."

IGGY POP

Mindfulness is a practice which involves being aware of ourselves and our surroundings and living in the present moment. It's learning to simply "be". When we do this we are engaged with life and able to live in harmony with ourselves and the environment.

Pay attention to your feelings.

Notice when something causes you distress, then find a way to change it.

Clutter can play a large part in how we feel in a space. It can distract our attention, create feelings of guilt and bombard our minds with excessive stimuli.

However, though clutter can cause a lot of stress in our lives it is also one of the easiest life stressors to fix, with the simple remedy of a little tidying up.

"You must live in the present, launch yourself on every wave, find your eternity in each moment. Fools stand on their island of opportunities and look toward another land. There is no other land; there is no other life but this."

HENRY DAVID THOREAU

Often the way in which we manifest ourselves in the physical world reflects our internal emotions and mental state. So if you are living in a mess it might suggest you have some things you need to work through.

Practise being in the moment

Take an apple and place it in front of you.

Spend five minutes taking in everything about this piece of fruit.

Consider its size, shape, any interesting markings, the colour and how it smells.

Close your eyes for a minute and recreate the image of the apple in your mind.

Think about how it would feel to hold, bite and taste the apple. Open your eyes and allow yourself to take a bite.

Chew mindfully and savour every moment of this experience.

When we engage with something properly, we live in the moment and take everything in. We feel, see and appreciate the experience more fully, so every second becomes memorable. This also makes us less likely to cram our world with superficial things because our life is already full and *meaningful*.

"In the midst of movement and chaos, keep stillness inside of you."

DEEPAK CHOPRA

Take a moment for yourself

Stop to be present in a moment and enjoy the feeling of time passing you without worrying.

Mindful awareness

Mindfulness can help us appreciate the smallest, most mundane task by reminding us that every choice or action delivers a result.

If we consider things that we do every day without thought – for example switching on a light, turning on a tap – we can see that each thing, however small, provides us with an outcome: the light comes on and illuminates the room, water pours freely from the tap.

If we then turn this attention to the practice of cleaning and tidying, we can see and appreciate the rewards.

We know that every little movement is leading us towards the final outcome, which serves to fire the enthusiasm and motivate us further.

"You can become blind by seeing each day as a similar one. Each day is a different one, each day brings a miracle of its own. It's just a matter of paying attention to this miracle."

PAULO COELHO

Accept what is,
let go of what was,
and have faith in what will be.

Pick one activity that will help you clear the clutter, for example stacking books on a bookshelf. As you embark on this activity, notice how you feel emotionally and physically.

Pay attention to how each muscle feels as you lift and stretch to put the books in place. Consider the amazing job that your body does, allowing you to move in this way.

Feel the energy involved as you move through the task and embrace it.

Immerse yourself fully in the activity and notice how that makes you feel.

Focusing on every part of the process brings the experience to life, making it more enjoyable.

Get into the habit of doing this every day with at least one task and it will help you see the mundane in a new and more magical light.

Tidiness and energy

Created over 3,000 years ago in China, the ancient art of feng shui looks at balancing the energies of a space to ensure better health, well-being and good fortune in almost any area. According to experts, feng shui improves and balances the flow of energy in the home, eliminating any areas where negative energy might be amplified or stagnant.

Practitioners first like to establish a sense of order and clarity. This is called the void and it is from this point that all good energy can flow. The best way to create a void is to clear the clutter until you have a blank canvas from which you can work.

"Your body is the temporary temple of your Spirit. What you keep around you in the extended temple of your home needs to change as you change and grow, so that it reflects who you are. Particularly if you are engaged in any kind of self-improvement work, you need to update your environment regularly. So get into the habit of leaving a trail of discarded clutter in your wake, and start to think of it as a sign of your progression!"

KAREN KINGSTON

Nothing changes,
if nothing changes.

Top tips for good energy

- Ensure that all entrances are kept clear of clutter. This includes bags, shoes, umbrellas and anything else that might have been left there during the day. Discarded items act as blocks to the flow of energy. Clearing space near any type of entrance provides a passage, allowing positive energy to flow into the home.

- Clear out store cupboards and spare bedrooms. A storeroom filled with junk blocks the flow of energy throughout the home. This causes a heavy atmosphere and feelings of confusion. Instead, invest in storage cupboards or boxes where you can keep things neat, organized and out of sight.

- Imagine each room has a swirling vortex of energy spinning through it. Is there room for it to spin easily, or will its passage be blocked by junk and clutter? Survey the room as an outsider would, then start tidying from the outside and work in so that all four corners are clear.

- Consider the central area of each room as a focal point where energy can gather and build, and allow space for this by keeping it clear, or mark it with a simple circular rug or mat.

- Keep windows and ledges clean and clear away any clutter. This allows light to illuminate the room and also means you can look out at the world, giving a sense of space and room to think and breathe.

> *"The best time for planning a book is while you're doing the dishes."*

AGATHA CHRISTIE

Untidiness creates a sense of chaos and disorder. It weighs on the body, mind and soul until you cannot lift your thoughts. To be creative you need to be flexible and free of baggage so that your mind can soar.

*"Eliminate physical clutter.
More importantly, eliminate
spiritual clutter."*

D.H. MONDFLEUR

Wa translates literally from Japanese to English as 'harmony'.

To be aware of your *Wa*, your own inner harmony, is to be in touch with yourself. When your *Wa* is disturbed you do not feel right and should do something to rectify it. Sometimes our *Wa* can be distrupted by the spaces we live or work in.

To be mindful is to live in awareness, having a tidy mind and allowing for a balanced *Wa*.

"A dream is your creative vision for your life in the future. You must break out of your current comfort zone and become comfortable with the unfamiliar and the unknown."

DENIS WAITLEY

It always seems impossible
until it's done.

Tidy schedule

Tidy up your daily schedule to allow yourself time to engage with your creative spirit.

Start by identifying when your brain is most active. For some people this is first thing in the morning; for others, later in the day or early evening.

Set some time aside during this period every day to simply sit and allow your imagination to run free.

Daydream about the future, make up stories about how you'd like your life to be, or just take in the view. It may seem like you're doing nothing, but these moments of stillness provide the soil from which creative thought grows.

If you practise this regularly you'll find that you can use the time more effectively, for problem solving, generating new ideas and stretching the imagination. If you find you're struggling to fit this in, take a look at the other activities that take up your time and see where you can cut back.

Streamline your day and clear the clutter, just as you would eliminate any unwanted junk from your home, to make your life work for you.

*"Time is a created thing.
To say 'I don't have time'
is to say 'I don't want to'."*

LAO TZU

When we create space we create time.

We are able to go with the flow,
rather than fighting against a sea
of confusion and chaos.

Utilize the space you have for simple storage solutions. Use the space under your bed, but instead of just shoving everything under there, keep things in boxes, baskets and purpose-made under-bed storage.

Be mindful that just because it is out of sight, doesn't mean it's out of mind.

> *"Have nothing in your house that you do not know to be useful, or believe to be beautiful."*

WILLIAM MORRIS

"The proper study of mankind is man in his relation to his deity."

D.H. LAWRENCE

Ancient civilizations understood the importance of order and tidiness and sought this perfection through their deities. In mythologies around the world there are an array of gods and goddesses responsible for clearing clutter, both physically and mentally, maintaining balance in heaven and on earth.

The ancient Egyptians believed everything had a place in the world. They were governed by order in their everyday routines. The goddess Maat was the personification of cosmic order and could help find structure in any area of life. She was responsible for judging the souls of the dead and putting them in their rightful place, depending on the weight of their deeds. She also maintained the natural order of things in heaven and on earth and ensured the passing of each season and the motion of the stars in the sky. A natural organizer, Maat is the mistress of tidiness.

The Greek goddess Hygieia was associated with maintaining good health, in addition to tidiness and purity. Even in ancient times, humans understood the connection between tidiness and well-being. Hygieia was the daughter of Asclepius, the Greek god of healing.

Aequitas is the Roman goddess of balance and fairness. A dignified deity, she was known for keeping order. Often pictured holding a set of scales and wearing a diadem, she appears on Roman coins and is also linked to abundance and wealth. This is because of her ability to organize and keep a tidy financial house! Aequitas is proof that efficient organization reaps rewards on many levels.

Take inspiration from the deities and visualise a giant set of scales in front of you.

Imagine all the joy of the world in one pan of the scales, and on the other side all the debris you've collected that you no longer need.

See how this weighs down the scales, making life heavy and laboured.

Now imagine removing everything you don't need, leaving only the things that mean something. Slowly the scales rise until they become level and provide balance in every area of your life.

The folklore of tidiness: Customs and traditions from around the world

Many Eastern countries have a number of customs relating to tidiness and order. On visiting someone's home, it's traditional to remove one's shoes before entering. This is a matter of respect and cleanliness. It's thought that if you don't remove your shoes, you could drag in dirt, which is akin to bringing bad luck into the home. It's also considered messy and shows a lack of respect.

In the gypsy or Roma tradition it's important to uphold what's known as the universal balance. This is called *kuntari,* and the ethos behind it is that everything must have its natural place in the world. Fish swim, birds fly, and if they can't then this puts everything out of order. The Roma also believe that they can become polluted. If this happens they're considered out of balance and have to go to trial. The outcome is usually a period of isolation away from the rest of the group.

"*A new broom sweeps clean,
but the old broom knows the corners.*"

IRISH PROVERB

In Britain, ancient civilizations used the broom as more than just a cleaning tool. They considered the act of sweeping away the clutter a means by which to remove negative energy and allow abundance to flow into the home. It was also thought that if a broom fell over then company was coming in the form of a surprise visitor!

*"By fairy hands their knell is rung;
By forms unseen their dirge is sung."*

WILLIAM COLLINS

According to folklore, the wee folk are partial to a clean and tidy house – in particular, the kitchen must be organized and in good order. Fairies don't like stacks of rubbish left in corners or things half finished. There's even a specific type of fairy called a brownie who inhabits a house and becomes responsible for cleaning and tidying it. Tiny wizened creatures with the appearance of an old man, brownies prefer to work at night unseen, and offer their domestic services in return for gifts of food or honey. Though brownies tend to hail from Scotland, the English version is called a hob and has the same role.

"Scrub and polish,— sweep and clean, —
Fling your windows wide!
See, the trees are clad in green!
Coax the spring inside!
Home, be shining fair to-day
For the guest whose name is May!"

LOUISE BENNETT WEAVER
AND HELEN COWLES LECRON

Green ingredients

Try to introduce green ingredients to your cleaning routine.

- Lemon juice – an acid that cuts through grease. Also use squeezed halves to wipe over surfaces to disinfect and clean. It is best to use fresh lemons here.

- Baking soda – an alkali and verstaile cleaner. Can be used neat or dissolved in water or vinegar which produces a fizz that speeds up the cleaning process.

- Vinegar – an acid and very versatile. It is a natural and safe disinfectant and can be used to tackle limescale and tough stains.

"We are used to cleaning the outside house, but the most important house to clean is yourself – your own house – which we never do."

MARINA ABRAMOVIC

Spring cleaning

It's a common tradition for people to practise 'spring cleaning'. It's thought that once the dreary long nights of winter are over and the first dewy buds appear, so the rubber gloves and duster should make their entrance too.

It's easy to see why this practice is popular; after being cooped up in the warm, stagnating in winter woollies, it's time to emerge, greet the sunlight and let fresh air into our homes.

Ancient civilizations also practised this behaviour. Their homes were lit by candles and fuelled by logs and coal, so it would have been a welcome relief to dust away the cobwebs and let the sweet spring breeze work its magic.

It's believed that the tradition of spring cleaning finds its origins in the Jewish custom of Passover, which falls every April. During this period the house would be cleaned and tidied from top to bottom, as families remembered the exodus of the Jews from Egypt.

These Jews, and those who were slaves, survived on unleavened bread and this has become an important symbol during the Passover holiday.

Keeping leavened bread in the house at Passover is seen as a great insult. Even errant crumbs that might have escaped can cause offence, hence the need for a good tidy, just to be sure that everything is spick and span.

"The Mole had been working very hard all the morning, spring-cleaning his little home. First with brooms, then with dusters; then on ladders and steps and chairs, with a brush and a pail of whitewash; till he had dust in his throat and eyes, and splashes of whitewash all over his black fur, and an aching back and weary arms. Spring was moving in the air above and in the earth below and around him, penetrating even his dark and lowly little house with its spirit of divine discontent and longing."

KENNETH GRAHAME

his is, *that tidiness is a*
sort of thing; why, tidiness
giants. You can't tidy
ithout untidying yourself..."

G.K. CHESTERTON

 Spring clean

The arrival of spring is the perfect opportunity to reorganize, declutter and clean.

Review what you have and have not used in the past 6 months. Consider a life without the things you have not used. How does it feel?

Tackle your wardrobe and bookshelves first. Are there any unwanted books, DVDs or CDs? Are there clothes you have never worn? Bag them up to either sell or give away to charity.

Once you have decluttered, it is time to clean. Open the windows, dust the shelves and thoroughly vacuum, making sure you pay attention to all those forgotten corners.

Seasonal cues

Allow the seasons to gently prompt
you to de-clutter your home and reflect
on your habits of consumption.

The C

There's
That's n
A scent
A whir as

There's so
In the colo
That's in th
Before the s

And though,
'Tis winter, w
There's somet
That winter's l

" Rum idea
timid, quiet
is a toil for
anything w

Seasonal cues

Allow the seasons to gently prompt
you to de-clutter your home and reflect
on your habits of consumption.

The Coming of the Spring

There's something in the air
That's new and sweet and rare –
A scent of summer things,
A whir as if of wings.

There's something, too, that's new
In the colour of the blue
That's in the morning sky,
Before the sun is high.

And though, on plain and hill,
'Tis winter, winter still,
There's something seems to say
That winter's had its day.

NORA PERRY

"Rum idea this is, that tidiness is a timid, quiet sort of thing; why, tidiness is a toil for giants. You can't tidy anything without untidying yourself..."

G.K. CHESTERTON

It takes effort to be tidy,
but it is worth it.

*"Good order is the foundation
of all things."*

EDMUND BURKE

**Be tidy in all things:
heart, mind, body and soul**

Make this your ethos and your life
will be bigger, brighter and richer.

BIBLIOGRAPHY

Adam, Henry. *The Education of Henry Adams*
(privately published, 1907)

Bennett Weaver, Louise & Colwes LeCron, Helen. *A Thousand Ways
to Please a Husband: with Bettina's Best Recipes*
(A.L. Burt Company, 1917)

Chesterton, G.K. *Man Alive* (John Lane, 1912)

Collins, William. 'The Patriotic Dead'

Grahame, Kenneth. *The Wind in the Willows* (Methuen, 1908)

Hobb, Robin. *City of Dragons* (Harper Collins UK, 2013)

Kingston, Karen. *Clear Your Clutter with Feng Shui*
(Piatkus, Little Brown, 2017)

Kipling, Rudyard. 'The Glory of the Garden', in *A School History
of England* (Oxford at the Clarendon Press, 1911)

Kondo, Marie. *The Life-Changing Magic of Tidying*
(Vermillion, 2014)

Lamb, Charles & Mary. 'Cleanliness' (1820-1825)

Mahan, Julie. *Insights on Productivity: Ideas from Industry
Professionals for Getting More Done in the Workplace*
(Dawson Publishing, 2007)

Oates, Joyce Carol. 'A Women's Work', interview in *The New York
Times Magazine* (April 10th, 2009)

Perry, Nora. 'The Coming of the Spring' (1831-1896)

Rams, Dieter. 'Dieter Rams: As Little Design as Possible', interview in *Kinfolk* magazine, issue twenty three (7th March, 2017)

Rubin, Gretchen. *Happier at Home* (Two Roads, 2013)

Scalise, Christina. *365 Daily Do Its: Organizing Tips and Challenges to Help You Get (and Stay) Organized Throughout the Year.* (self published, 2016)

Shaw, George Bernard. 'Maxims for Revolutionists', in *Man and Superman* (1902)

Stein, Gertrude. *Reflection on the Atomic Bomb: The Previously Uncollected Writings of Gertrude Stein, Volume 1* (Black Sparrow Press, 1973)

Twain, Mark. *Following the Equator* (American Publishing Company, 1897)

Way Teal, Edwin. *The American Seasons* (Dodd, Mead & Co, 1976)

QUOTES ARE TAKEN FROM:

A. A. Milne was an English author best known for his books about Winnie-the-Pooh.

Agatha Christie was an English crime novelist, short-story writer and playwright.

Albert Einstein was a theoretical physicist. He is renowned for developing the general theory of relativity and received the Nobel Prize for Physics in 1921.

Baidurya Mukherjee is a poet.

Barbara Walters is an American broadcast journalist, author and television personality.

B.K.S. Iyengar was the founder of Iyengar Yoga and was considered one of the foremost yoga teachers in the world.

Brunello Cucinelli is an Italian fashion designer who set up the fashion brand named after him.

Charles Lamb was an English essayist and poet best known for his *Essays of Elia*.

Christina Scalise is an author and professional organizer.

David Hobson is an American gardener and comedian.

Deepak Chopra is an American author, public speaker and prominent figure in the New Age movement.

D.H. Lawrence was an author, who most famously wrote the controversial novel *Lady Chatterley's Lover*.

D.H. Mondfleur is a writer and advocate of minimalism.

Denis Waitley is an American motivational speaker and writer. He is the best-selling author of the audio series *The Psychology of Winning*.

Dieter Rams is a German industrial designer closely associated with the consumer products company Braun.

Edmund Burke was an Irish author, orator and pilosopher. He served as a member of parliament with the Whig party.

Edwin Way Teale was an American naturalist, photographer and Pulitzer prize-winning writer.

George Bernard Shaw was an Irish playwright who wrote more than 60 plays. He was awarded the Nobel Prize in Literature in 1925.

G.K. Chesterton was an English writer, philosopher and lay theologian.

Gertrude Stein was an American novelist and playwright during the first half on the 20th century.

Gretchen Rubin is an American author and speaker on happiness.

Helen Cowles LeCron wrote *A Thousand Ways to Please a Husband* with Louise Bennett Weaver.

Henry Brooks Adams was descended from two US presidents and was an American historian.

Henry David Thoreau was an American author and poet.

Hermann Hesse was a German poet and novelist. He was awarded the Nobel Prize for Literature in 1946.

Iggy Pop is an Amercian singer-songwriter.

James Naismith was a sports coach and innovator who invented the game of basketball in 1891.

Joan Baez is a contemporary US folk musician and activist for social justice.

John Updike was an American short-story writer and poet.

Joyce Carol Oates is an American author who has published over 40 novels.

Juan Felipe Herrera has been the US Poet Laureate since 2015.

Julia Cameron is an author and teacher, most famous for her book *The Artist's Way*.

Julie Mahan is the author of *Insights on Productivity*.

Karen Kingston is a top feng shui adviser.

Katherine Paterson is a Chinese-born American children's author.

Kenneth Grahame was a Scottish writer, well-known for his novel *The Wind in the Willows*.

Lao Tzu was a philosopher and poet of ancient China, best known for his work *Tao Te Ching*.

Leonardo da Vinci was an Italian polymath and is considered to be one of the greatest painters of all time.

Liberty Hyde Bailey was an American botanist and horticulturalist.

Louise Bennett Weaver wrote *A Thousand Ways to Please a Husband* with Helen Cowles LeCron.

Marie Kondo is a best-selling author and organization consultant.

Marina Abramovic is a Serbian perfomance artist.

Mark Twain (Samuel Langhorne Clemens) was an American author who wrote the *The Adventures of Huckleberry Finn*, often referred to as 'the great American novel'.

Mary Lamb was a British author who co-wrote *Tales From Shakespeare* with her brother Charles.

Napoleon Hill was an American self-help author in the 20th century.

Natalia Ginzburg was an American author interested in family relationships and politics.

Nora Perry was an American poet.

Paul Meyer is a french clarinettist.

Paulo Coelho is an international award-winning Brazilian novelist.

Peter Walsh is an Australian-American professional organizer, writer and media personality.

Publilius Syrus was a Syrian writer of the first century BCE, brought to Italy as a slave.

R.A. Salvatore is an award-winning American author.

Richard Wagner was a German composer and opera director.

Robin Hobb, pen name for Margaret Astrid Lindholm Ogden, is an American author.

Rudyard Kipling was an English author known most famously for *The Jungle Book*.

Sri Sathya Sai Baba was an Indian teacher, guru and charity worker.

Socrates was a classical Greek philosopher and the teacher of Plato.

Ursus Wehrli is a Swiss comedian, designer and artist.

William Collins was a Scottish teacher, editor and publisher.

William Morris was a British artist and poet, famed for his work in textiles.

William Ralph Inge was an Anglican priest and Dean of St Paul's Cathedral, London.

Winston Churchill was the British Prime Minister during the Second World War.

Viv Apple is a poet and author from Nottingham, UK.

FURTHER READING

Books

Christina Scalise. *365 Daily Do Its: Organizing Tips and Challenges to Help You Get (and Stay) Organized Throughout the Year* (self published, 2016)

Christina Scalise. *Organize Your Life and More!* (Brighton Publishing, 2012)

Kingston, Karen. *Clear your Clutter with Feng Shui* (Piatkus, 2008)

Kondo, Marie. *The Life-Changing Magic of Tidying: A Simple, Effective Way to Banish Clutter Forever* (Vermilion, 2014)

Sasaki, Fumio. *Goodbye, Things: On Minimalist Living* (Penguin, 2017)

Silverthorn, Vicky. *Start with Your Sock Drawer: The Simple Guide to Living a Less Cluttered Life* (Sphere, 2016)

Tatsumi, Nagisa. *The Art of Discarding: How to Get Rid of Clutter and Find Joy* (Yellow Kite, 2017)

Wallman, James. *Stuffocation: Living More with Less* (Penguin Life, 2017)

PAGE REFERENCES

Page 12: Way Teal, Edwin. *The American Seasons* (Dodd, Mead & Co, 1976)

Page 34: Kondo, Marie. *The Life-Changing Magic of Tidying* (Vermillion, 2014)

Page 42: Scalise, Christina. *365 Daily Do Its: Organizing Tips and Challenges to Help You Get (and Stay) Organized Throughout the Year.* (self published, 2016)

Page 44: Rubin, Gretchen. *Happier at Home* (Two Roads, 2013)

Page 47: Mahan, Julie. *Insights on Productivity: Ideas from Industry Professionals for Getting More Done in the Workplace* (Dawson Publishing, 2007)

Page 62: Stein, Gertrude. *Reflection on the Atomic Bomb: The Previously Uncollected Writings of Gertrude Stein, Volume 1* (Black Sparrow Press, 1973)

Page 66: Mahan, Julie. *Insights on Productivity: Ideas from Industry Professionals for Getting More Done in the Workplace* (Dawson Publishing, 2007)

Page 68: Twain, Mark. *Following the Equator* (American Publishing Company, 1897)

Page 80: Kipling, Rudyard. 'The Glory of the Garden', in *A School History of England* (Oxford at the Clarendon Press, 1911)

Page 91: Shaw, George Bernard. 'Maxims for Revolutionists', in *Man and Superman* (1902)

Page 96: Lamb, Charles & Mary. 'Cleanliness' (1820-1825)

Page 97: Hobb, Robin. *City of Dragons* (Harper Collins UK, 2013)

Page 108: 'A Women's Work', interview in *The New York Times Magazine* (April 10th, 2009)

Page 117: Adam, Henry. *The Education of Henry Adams* (privately published, 1907)

Page 121: 'Dieter Rams: As Little Design as Possible', interview in *Kinfolk* magazine, issue twenty three (7th March, 2017)

Page 140: Kingston, Karen. *Clear Your Clutter with Feng Shui* (Piatkus, Little Brown, 2017)

Page 166: Collins, William. 'The Patriotic Dead'

Page 168: Bennett Weaver, Louise & Colwes LeCron, Helen. *A Thousand Ways to Please a Husband: with Bettina's Best Recipes* (A.L. Burt Company, 1917)

Page 174: Grahame, Kenneth. *The Wind in the Willows* (Methuen, 1908)

Page 177: Perry, Nora. 'The Coming of the Spring' (1831-1896)

Page 178: Chesterton, G.K. *Man Alive* (John Lane, 1912)

Publishing Director Sarah Lavelle
Editor Harriet Butt
Editorial Assistant Harriet Webster
Creative Director Helen Lewis
Series Designer Emily Lapworth
Assistant Designer Shani Travers
Production Director Vincent Smith
Production Controller Nikolaus Ginelli

First published in 2017 by
Quadrille Publishing Ltd
52–54 Southwark Street
London SE1 1 UN
www.quadrille.com

Quadrille is an imprint of Hardie Grant
www.hardiegrant.com

Compilation, design and layout © 2017
Quadrille Publishing Ltd

Text on pages 5, 6, 7, 8, 11, 13, 15, 16, 17,
18, 19, 20, 21, 23, 25, 26, 27, 28, 29, 30, 31,
33, 35, 36, 37, 38, 39, 41, 43, 45, 46, 49, 50,
51, 56, 59, 60, 61, 63, 64, 65, 69, 71, 72, 74,
75, 77, 78, 81, 82, 83, 84, 85, 86, 88, 90, 92,
93, 94, 99, 101, 103, 107, 109, 111, 113, 114,
115, 116, 119, 123, 124, 125, 127, 128, 129,
131, 132, 133, 135, 136, 137, 138, 139, 141,
142, 143, 145, 147, 149, 150, 151, 153, 154,
157, 158, 159, 160, 161, 162, 163, 165, 167,
169, 171, 172, 173, 175, 176, 179 181
© 2017 Alison Davies

British Library Cataloguing-
in-Publication Data
A catalogue record for this book is
available from the British Library.

ISBN: 978 178713 113 2

Printed in China